W9-CHZ-181

Cheerleading FOR FUN!

By Beth Gruber

Content Adviser: Melissa Signor, Head Cheerleading Coach, Columbia University, New York, New York
Reading Adviser: Frances J. Bonacci, Reading Specialist, Cambridge, Massachusetts

COMPASS POINT BOOKS
MINNEAPOLIS, MINNESOTA

Compass Point Books
3109 West 50th Street, #115
Minneapolis, MN 55410

Visit Compass Point Books on the Internet at *www.compasspointbooks.com*
or e-mail your request to *custserv@compasspointbooks.com*

Photographs ©: Kwame Zikomo/SuperStock, front cover (left); Courtesy of Pep Threads, front cover (top right), 16, 17 (center); PhotoDisc, front cover (bottom right), 17 (bottom), 35, 42 (right), 43 (left and center), 45 (top), back cover; Lisette Le Bon/SuperStock, 5; Underwood & Underwood/Corbis, 7; Rubberball Productions, 9, 33, 43 (top and right); Tom Stewart/Corbis, 11; Getty Images, 13, 14-15; Courtesy of Kaepa, 17 (top); Garry Wade/Getty Images, 25; Trinette Reed/Corbis, 27; Ronald Martinez/Getty Images, 29; Duomo/Corbis, 31; Michael Krasowitz/Getty Images, 36-37; Paul Barton/Corbis, 38-39; Lindsay Hebberd/Corbis, 41; EyeWire, 42 (left); Gerry Wade/Getty Images, 44; Republican National Committee, 45 (bottom).

Editor: Sandra E. Will/Bill SMITH STUDIO
Photo Researchers: Sandra E. Will and Christie Silver/Bill SMITH STUDIO
Designers: Colleen Sweet and Brian Kobberger/Bill SMITH STUDIO

Library of Congress Cataloging-in-Publication Data

Gruber, Beth.
Cheerleading for fun / by Beth Gruber.
p. cm. – (Activities for fun)
Includes index.
Summary: An introduction to cheerleading, presenting the history of this activity, advice on tryouts, the necessary skills and techniques involved, information on camps and competitions, and more.
ISBN 0-7565-0584-4
1. Cheerleading–Juvenile literature. [1. Cheerleading.] I. Title.
II. Series.
LB3635.G78 2004
791.6'4—dc22 2003015820

Table of Contents

The Basics

INTRODUCTION/Cheerleading Is Fun! 4

THE FIRST CHEERLEADERS/
Rah, Ski-U-Mah, Hoorah! 6

READY, SET, CHEER/
So You Want to Be a Cheerleader 8

GETTING STARTED/Shaping Up 10

TACKLING TRYOUTS/Making the Squad 12

TRAINING TIME/Show Me How 14

GET IN GEAR/Looking Good 16

Doing It

BASIC MOVES/Give Us a Hand! 18

FIRST STEPS/Leg Work 20

JUMP TO IT/Lowdown on Jumps 22

STUNTING SAFELY/It Takes Teamwork 24

BOTTOM'S UP/Who's on Base? 26

HIGH FLYING/In the Air 28

SPOTTING/One Tough Job 30

IN FORMATION/Take Your Position 32

People, Places, and Fun

CHEERS AND CHANTS/
Let's Hear It for the Team 34

WE'VE GOT SPIRIT/Reasons to Cheer 36

CHEERLEADING CAMPS/Summertime Fun 38

CHEERLEADING COMPETITIONS/
The Ones to Watch 40

CHEERLEADING TIMELINE/
What Happened When? 42

TRIVIA/Cheerleading Chart Toppers 44

QUICK REFERENCE GUIDE/
Cheerleading Words to Know 46

GLOSSARY/Other Words to Know 47

WHERE TO LEARN MORE 47

INDEX 48

Note: In this book, there are two kinds of vocabulary words. Cheerleading Words to Know are words specific to cheerleading. They are in **bold** and are defined on page 46. Other Words to Know are helpful words that aren't related only to cheerleading. They are ***bold and italicized.*** These are defined on page 47.

Cheerleading Is Fun!

You can see it in the glowing smile that cheerleaders wear whenever they perform.

It's a smile that's catching and makes sports fans stand up and cheer. It sends a message of support to the home team. It's a reminder to every member of the **squad** of the good times they have had making new friends, sharing new experiences, and celebrating victory. It shows that it's fun to wow the crowd with dance moves, **stunts,** tumbling, and cheers.

Most of all, a cheerleader's smile shows confidence, team spirit, and pride.

Do you know any cheerleaders? In this book, you will learn more about the spirit, strength, and moves that make cheerleading such a popular activity.

Rah, Ski-U-Mah, Hoorah!

It was a cold day on November 2, 1898, at the University of Minnesota, and football fans were not smiling. The home team was losing, and things looked grim.

Then, a tremendous roar made the crowd sit up and pay attention. Six male college students, led by Johnny Campbell, had run onto the field. They were cheering for the home team with all of their might. They called themselves the Yell Captains, and they were America's first official cheerleaders.

They stood before the crowd and yelled, "Rah, Rah, Rah! Ski-U-Mah! Hoorah! Hoorah! **Varsity!** Varsity! Minnesota!" Soon the crowd joined in and cheered the home team to victory.

Male cheerleaders from Yale University perform a routine during a football game in 1930.

During the 1920s, cheerleading began to include gymnastics and tumbling. At this time, women were invited to become cheerleaders, too. Then, in the 1940s, American men were called to fight in World War II. Cheerleading changed overnight. Suddenly, it was women, not men, who were leading the cheers at sports events across the country.

Shaping Up

Cheerleaders need strength, ***endurance***, and ***flexibility*** to perform their best. To build endurance, try jumping rope, jumping jacks, or jogging to get in shape. You might try putting on some music and moving to the rhythm. Count the beats in the music as you move.

Stretching and strength-training exercises are important, too. Let a coach or trainer show you how to get started.

Stretching helps prevent muscle injury and gives your body the flexibility to perform tough moves. Take the time to stretch from head to toe. Be sure to stretch all the major muscle groups, including the legs, arms, shoulders, and back. Hold each stretch for 20 to 30 seconds, then repeat a second time. Do not bounce!

Push-ups and ***abdominal crunches*** are excellent strength-training exercises.

Remember, you'll need to train your voice for cheerleading, too. Practice breathing deeply and yelling in a low, clear voice. Use your whole chest, not just your throat, for power. You can do it!

Working out with friends is a fun way to get in shape. Many cheerleaders work out at the gym with their team members or friends.

Making the Squad

Does your school have a cheerleading squad? If so, most cheerleading squads hold **tryouts** in the spring. This allows the new squad plenty of time to work together before the school year ends. They might even schedule some time at a cheerleading camp (see pg. 38) during the summer months.

Make sure you know when your school holds its cheerleading tryouts. Ask a lot of questions. Coaches and current cheerleaders will be able to tell you what to practice. They might even suggest exercises to help you get in shape for tryouts.

Many squads schedule a **practice week** before the real tryouts begin. Practice week allows students who want to cheer plenty of time to learn the stunts, routines, cheers, and chants upon which they will be judged. It also allows the coaches time to teach key skills and to get a good look at students who will be trying out.

At the tryout, cheerleaders will be judged on spirit, cheer motions, jumps, timing and rhythm, motions, voice ***projection,*** and overall performance. So, look sharp and go for it!

Tryout Day Tips

Wear attractive, snug-fitting clothes.

If your hair is long, keep it tied back in a ponytail.

Smile.

Use a loud voice and pronounce each cheer clearly.

If you make a mistake, ask to try again.

Show Me How

It's not surprising that many coaches were once cheerleaders themselves. They know the moves. They know how to keep a squad in top form. They know how to make hard work fun!

Most coaches are trained by one of these four organizations: the American Association of Cheerleading Coaches and Advisors, the National Cheerleaders Association, the Universal Cheerleaders Association, or the International Cheerleading Foundation.

Many top coaches never ask their squads to do anything they wouldn't do themselves. Coaches are responsible for more than just the skills and routines a squad performs. They are also responsible for

designing and monitoring a squad's **conditioning** program, for preventing injury, and for keeping team spirit high. Sometimes that means helping squad members resolve conflicts, or problems. Other times it means helping cheerleaders overcome fears that prevent them from performing a particular stunt.

Many coaches encourage their squads to try new moves and help them perfect difficult stunts and routines. A good coach always wants what is best for the team.

Looking Good

Cheerleaders like to look their best. They want to be prepared and look good, whether they're practicing or at an event.

For practice, cheerleaders choose tight-fitting shorts or pants and a snug top. These clothes make it easier for **spotters** to catch cheerleaders safely if they fall.

At games and events, cheerleaders wear uniforms in their school or squad colors. Females wear short skirts and form-fitting shells or sweaters. Male cheerleaders typically wear shorts or pants and a shirt in school colors.

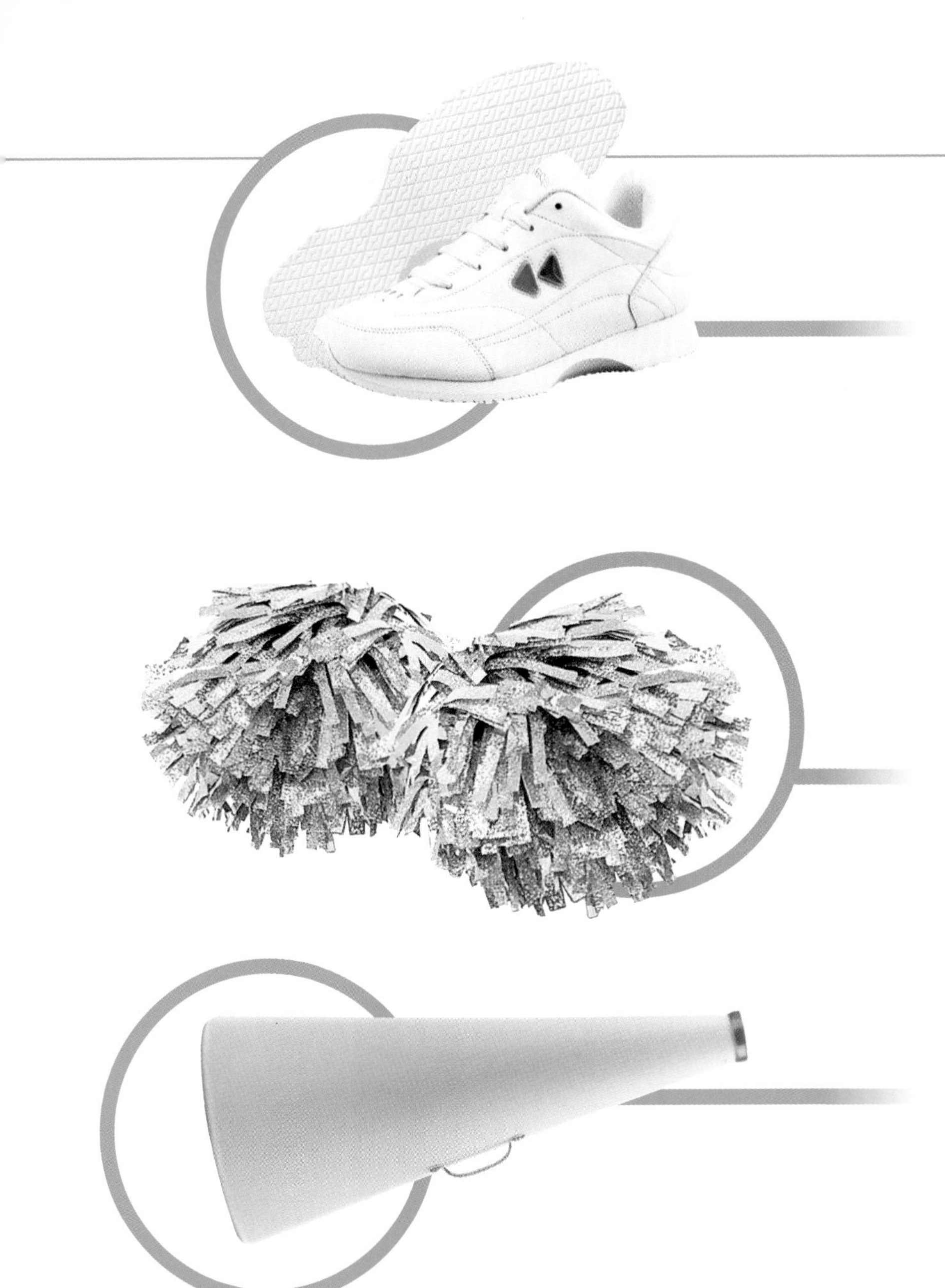

Well-designed athletic shoes suited for jumping and tumbling help cheerleaders perform their routines and stunts. Look for shoes that are comfortable, supportive, and lightweight.

Pompoms are used to grab the crowd's attention. Pompoms are made of plastic strips, and they come in a variety of colors.

Megaphones are used to emphasize voices and lead the crowd in cheers.

Give Us a Hand!

Do you ever wonder how cheerleaders memorize so many tricky moves? It's easier than it looks! Most moves begin with the same hand, arm, and leg motions. Cheerleaders learn the basics first. Then, they mix them up and make their own moves.

Here are some of the basic moves used in cheerleading:

Blades: In this move, cheerleaders extend their arms from their shoulders in a straight line without bending their wrists. They keep their hands open flat with their fingers pressed tightly together and their thumbs tucked inward.

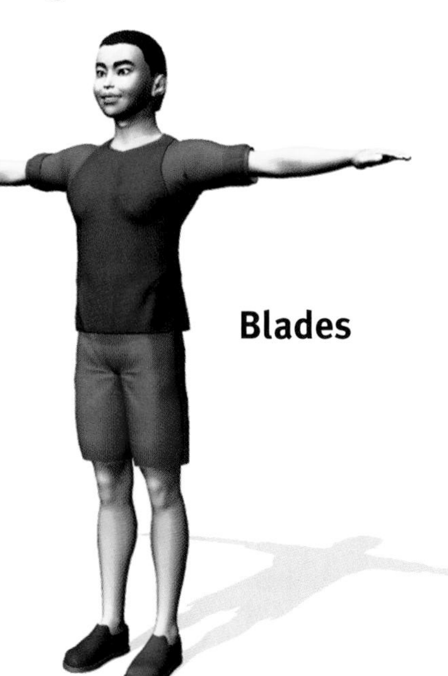

Blades

Daggers: To make a dagger, cheerleaders bend their arms at the elbow and tuck their elbows into their sides. Then, they keep both fists pressed tightly against their shoulders with the pinky side of the fist facing forward.

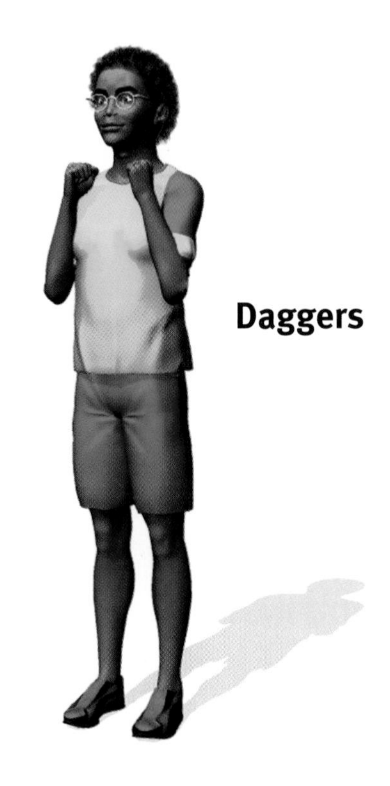

Daggers

High V

High V: In this move, cheerleaders raise their arms straight above their head. They extend their arms wide to look like the letter "V." To do a low V, cheerleaders bring their arms down so the "V" is upside down.

Leg Work

Once cheerleaders know some basic hand and arm motions, they add some leg work. These easy moves are a great place for cheerleaders to start:

Forward Lunge: To begin the lunge, cheerleaders place their fists on their hips and move one leg straight back, while bending the front leg. In order to prevent injury, cheerleaders must be sure to keep the knee of the bent leg aligned (in line) with the ankle.

Forward Lunge

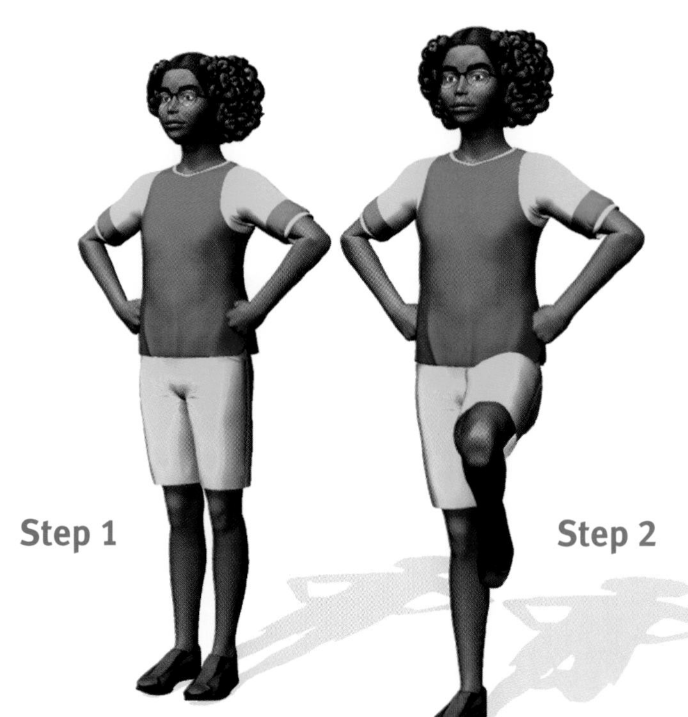

Left Liberty

Left or Right Liberty: First, cheerleaders stand straight with fists on their hips. Then, they bend their left leg and lift up their foot until the left foot rests against the side of the right knee. Next, they point their left foot down, while keeping the right leg perfectly straight. For a right liberty, they perform the same movements with their right leg.

Lowdown on Jumps

How do cheerleaders learn to jump so high? They practice. The best jumpers practice every day. For safety, they always have an adult spotter (see pg. 30) with them. Before cheerleaders practice, they stretch and warm up. Stretching and warming up are especially important for jumps, because jumping uses every part of the body.

Prep

The first part of a jump is called the "prep." Its purpose is to power the body off the ground. Cheerleaders begin with feet together and hands by their sides. In a single motion, they quickly swing both arms into a high V position and lift onto their toes.

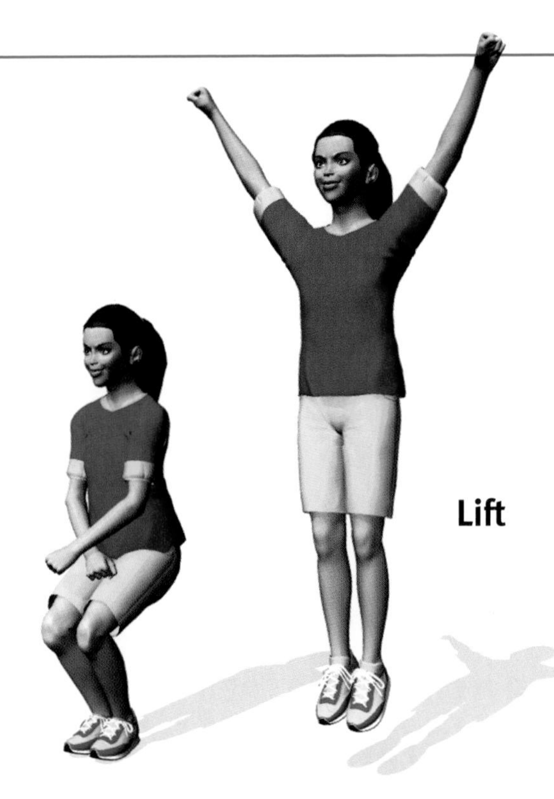

Next, they swing both arms down and across the body, bending both knees and keeping their body tight. Then, they bring both of their arms back up into a high V. As they raise their arms, they push off with their legs and use their toes to get as high as possible. This is called the "lift."

Last comes the "landing." At the highest point of the jump, cheerleaders whip both of their legs together and bend their knees slightly to absorb the ***impact*** of hitting the ground. Finally, they land on the balls of their feet and roll back on their heels.

It Takes Teamwork

Great stunts are what set cheerleading squads apart from the crowd. They're cool! They're exciting! They are also more dangerous than they look!

When a team warms up for stunt practice, they might try a game that builds trust among the squad members. For instance, they might have all but one squad member sit in a circle with their legs straight out in front of them. The last cheerleader stands in the center of the circle with his or her arms folded across the chest. Everyone's feet should be positioned tightly against the standing cheerleader's ankles. Then, the standing cheerleader falls backwards into the circle. People in the circle use both feet to catch the cheerleader and toss him or her from person to person. Cheerleaders take turns in the center position. Remember! You should not try these moves without adult supervision.

When Trying Stunts

Cheerleaders and their coaches talk through every stunt so that everyone knows exactly what they are going to be doing. There is nothing more dangerous than a cheerleader asking, "What are we doing?" in the middle of a stunt!

When practicing stunts, cheerleaders always make sure that they have a spotter on hand and adult supervision.

Who's on Base?

Three key positions are critical in stunting: the bases, the flyers, and the spotters. The bases support the bottom of the stunt. They provide the ***foundation*** on which the flyer (see pg. 28) will perform tricks and moves.

To prevent injury, bases should lift with their legs and arms, not with their backs. Bases position themselves in a straight line. Their knees should be slightly bent, arms tucked in close to the body, and backs straight. Looking forward helps keep their backs in proper position.

They line up so the gap between each base is no more than shoulder width. Bases should hold their bodies "rock steady."

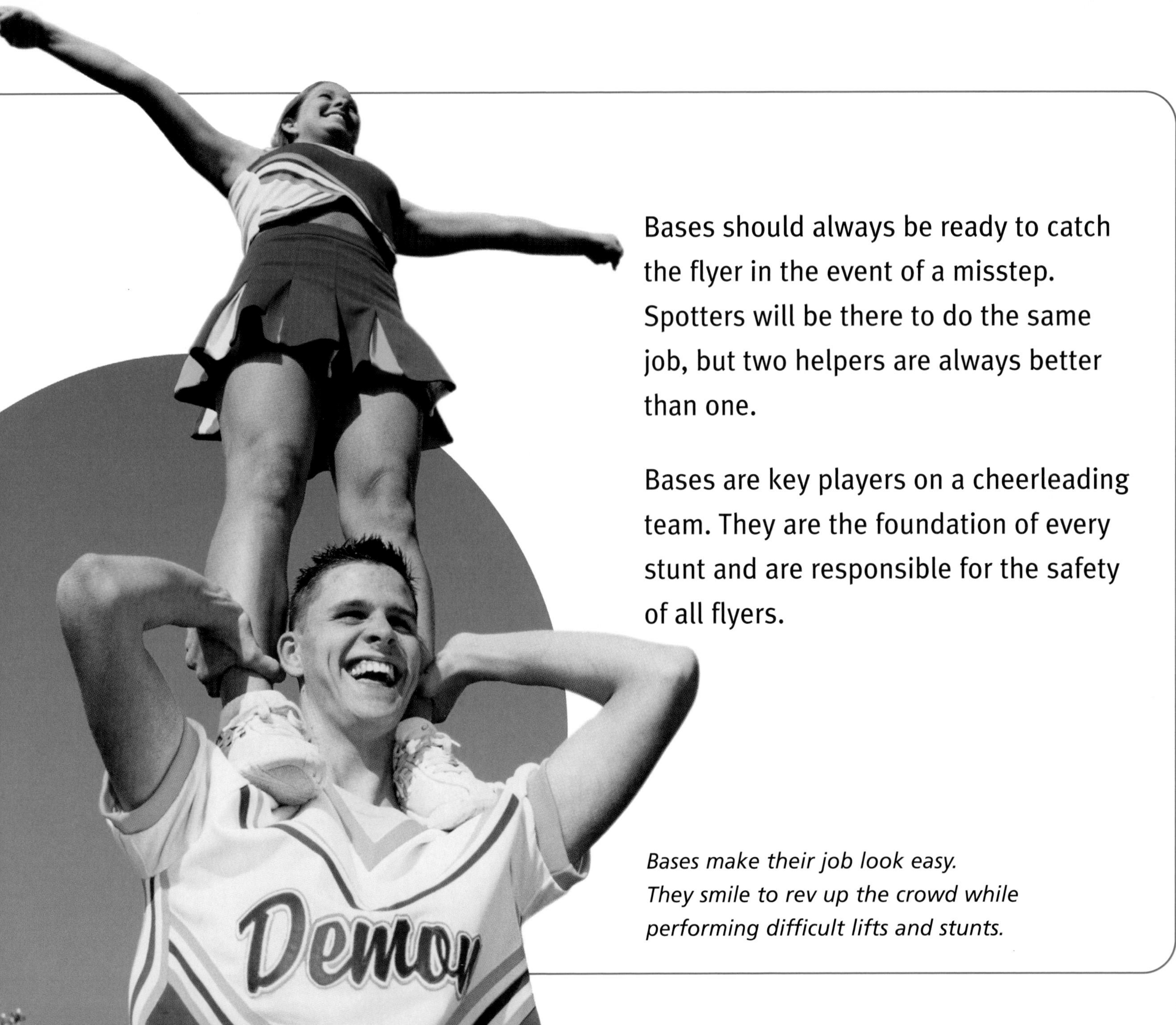

Bases should always be ready to catch the flyer in the event of a misstep. Spotters will be there to do the same job, but two helpers are always better than one.

Bases are key players on a cheerleading team. They are the foundation of every stunt and are responsible for the safety of all flyers.

Bases make their job look easy. They smile to rev up the crowd while performing difficult lifts and stunts.

In the Air

The flyer is the second key position in a stunt. The best flyers are able to control their body positions in the air and stay very tight, like a board. They perform the top or ***aerial*** part of the stunt.

Flying is fun, but it can also be a little scary. To move through the air safely, flyers tuck their bodies in tightly when going up and coming down. They must remember to make their bodies as compact as possible. This means keeping their arms and legs close to the body. This makes the stunt a lot safer, even if it fails.

Flyers need to be strong, just like the bases, to support their own body weight. Push-ups and ***weight lifting*** help flyers build the arm strength they need to support their bodies completely.

Some types of aerial stunts, such as this one, are only allowed in college-level cheerleading.

Good flyers make stunts look easy. At the top of the stunt, they are confident, make plenty of eye contact with the crowd, and smile. They remember to keep all the moves sharp, just like they practiced them on the ground.

One Tough Job

The third key position in any stunt is the spotter. These strong athletes must keep their attention focused at all times and be available to help wherever help is needed.

Sometimes, they need to steady the bases if they seem unstable. Other times, spotters need to catch the flyers if they are falling. At all times, they need to watch every part of a stunt carefully and know how to fix things if something goes wrong.

It is important for spotters to keep their eyes and hands on the flyer whenever possible. This helps brace the stunt and also makes the flyer feel more secure. If a flyer does fall, the spotter always tries to protect the flyer's head and neck first to prevent serious injury.

Not everyone can base, fly, or spot. Stunting takes teamwork. Each member of the team must take the job the coach assigns and give it their all!

Cheerleaders often use many spotters for each stunt to ensure the safety of the flyer. The difficulty of the stunt determines the number of spotters needed.

Take Your Position

Formations are the foundation of the most spectacular cheerleading routines. The most familiar formation is the **pyramid.** There are many formations a squad can do to mix things up a little and give a more exciting performance. For more dramatic formations, a coach might add **handsprings, cartwheels,** stunts, and transitions. The crowd will love it!

One basic formation is called a 3/4/4. Each number represents how many cheerleaders will be in that row. For example, three people might kneel in the first row. Four people might lunge in the second row. Everyone in the third row might stand up tall and hit a high V position with their arms.

The basic triangle formation lends itself especially well to **ripples,** level changes, and a variety of cool stunts. The diamond formation also lends itself well to ripples.

There are formations for 10-person squads, 15-person squads, and even squads of 20 or larger. It helps if a squad is creative when deciding which formations to perform. Even the most ordinary formations look exciting when stunts and original moves are added to them.

The thigh stand is a common formation used in squads of all sizes.

Let's Hear It for the Team

Do you know the difference between a chant and a cheer?

A chant is short. It is repeated multiple times. Chants have an easy beat for the crowd to follow. Cheerleaders use different hand and leg movements, or even pompoms, to keep chants and cheers exciting. Here are some popular chants used by cheerleaders from schools across the country. Try them!

Stand up crowd,
It's time to shout.
Come on fans,
Yell it out.

One, two, three, four,
(Your team's name)
Raise that score!

Cheers are a little longer than chants, and they are said only once. There are **crowd cheers, show cheers,** and **mount cheers.** Cheerleaders use lots of movements to make them more fun!

You know you can depend on us to get the job done
'Cause when it comes to (team sport),
we are number one!
Say the number: one
Say it louder: one
We are the proud: one
You got it...number one!

Hi! Hello! How do you do?
We are the (team name) and we welcome you.
We stand proud for the (school colors).
We wish you well. Good luck to you!

Reasons to Cheer

It takes a huge amount of spirit to be a good cheerleader. All cheerleaders have it, and they know how to spread it around.

If school spirit is down in the dumps, count on the cheerleading squad to boost ***morale*** with fun pep rallies designed to make everyone feel good.

Cheerleaders have the unique ability to gather support for important causes, both on and off the field. Is there a local community project that needs volunteers or money? Canned food drives, community cleanups, and recycling efforts are just a few of the ways cheerleaders can help build better communities by generating ***enthusiasm*** and getting everyone involved.

Remember that being a cheerleader is not just about cheering. It's about being a leader, too. Pick projects carefully. Check with the coach to organize squad time. Make sure every cheerleader has a job to do. Then, take a good look around. Cheerleaders who make a positive difference in the lives of others have lots of reasons to cheer!

Cheerleaders can help build better communities, on and off the field.

Summertime Fun

The school year may be over, but for many cheerleaders, cheerleading camp means the work has just begun.

Cheerleading camp is a terrific place to make new friends and learn new skills. It's an opportunity to see what other cheerleaders are doing. It's a time when squads learn to bond and think like a team. First-timers learn confidence and basic moves they will use all year.

Make sure you are ready for your first visit to camp. Build up your flexibility and strength before you go. Make a list of things you would like to learn. Get ready for long days of super-challenging work. Don't forget to pack a camera and a smile: You will want to remember the fun you've had when cheerleading camp is through!

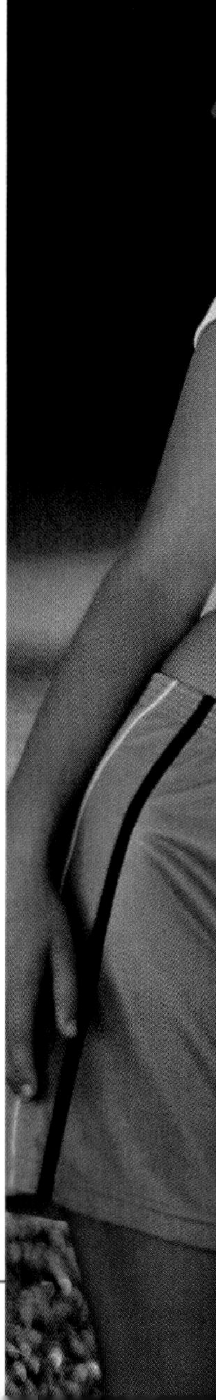

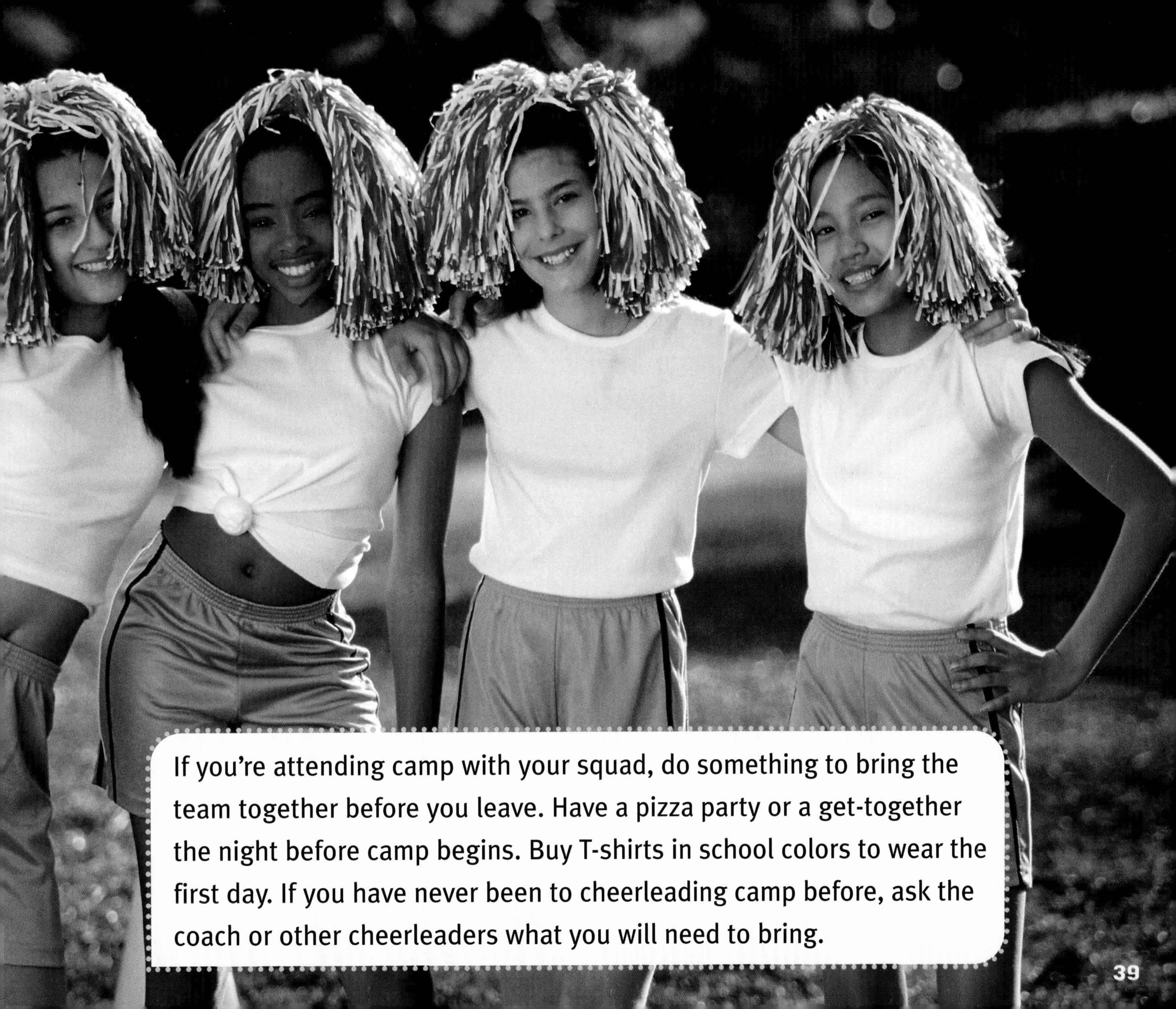

If you're attending camp with your squad, do something to bring the team together before you leave. Have a pizza party or a get-together the night before camp begins. Buy T-shirts in school colors to wear the first day. If you have never been to cheerleading camp before, ask the coach or other cheerleaders what you will need to bring.

The Ones to Watch

What does it take to be a winner? Watch some cheerleading ***competitions*** to find out. Take note. Are the stunts perfectly executed with no mistakes? Are the formations original and unique? Are the cheers fresh and new? Does the team perform well together? Do they look neat and professional? Do they have enormous energy?

Competitions are a big part of cheerleading, whether local or national. The National Cheerleaders Association hosts more than 20 championship events around the country throughout the year. Watch the Universal Cheerleaders Association Championships (usually carried on television) to see the hottest stunts and top cheerleaders from a variety of age groups.

Competitions can be a fun, exciting, and stressful time for cheerleaders, coaches, and fans. The squads that bring a positive attitude and do the best they can do are all truly winners, no matter how they score!

NCA

What Happened When?

776 1900 1920 1930 1940 1950

776 B.C. Ancient Greeks cheer for their favorite runners at the first Olympic games.

1880 The first organized, reported yell is performed at a college football game in Princeton, New Jersey.

1898 Medical student Johnny Campbell and the Yell Captains introduce cheerleading at a University of Minnesota football game.

1900s Gamma Sigma, the first cheerleading ***fraternity,*** is established. The megaphone becomes a popular cheerleading instrument.

1919 Shirley Windsor organizes a pep rally at the University of Kansas. He (yes, Shirley was a guy) raises enough money to build a brand-new stadium for his school.

1920s "Just Yells," the first book about cheerleading, is published.

1923 Female students are invited to cheer for the first time anywhere at the University of Minnesota.

1930s Cheerleaders add a new twist to their performance—paper pompoms.

1939–1945 Women begin to dominate cheerleading as young men are fighting in World War II.

1940s Lawrence R. Herkimer forms the first cheerleading company. The first national association for cheerleaders, the American Cheerleaders Association, is established.

1950 The National Cheerleaders Association is established.

1954 Herkimer presents the very first **spirit stick** at a cheerleading camp. It is made from a painted tree branch.

1957 The National Cheerleaders Association introduces the first mass-manufactured spirit sticks.

1960 1970 1980 1990 2000

1960 The Baltimore Colts football team introduces the first professional cheerleading squad.

1967 The Top 10 college cheer squads are ranked for the first time.

1970s Training for cheerleading coaches is first offered at summer cheerleading camps.

1971 The International Cheerleading Foundation creates the "Cheerleader All America" awards for outstanding sportsmanship in cheerleading.

1972 The Dallas Cowboys cheerleaders make their first appearance.

1978 CBS-TV televises the first national broadcast of the National Collegiate Cheerleading Championships.

1980s National cheerleading competitions for junior and senior high schools are held across the country. Cheerleaders receive national media recognition for school and community leadership.

1982 Cheerleading makes an international splash in Great Britain, Germany, Sweden, and Japan.

1983 ESPN broadcasts its first National Collegiate Cheerleading Championships.

1995 American Cheerleader magazine and Cheers and More newsletter are first published.

1998 The Cheerleading Alliance is founded.

2000 The Cheerleading Alliance changes its name to the Cheer and Dance Alliance. Cheerleaders do a cheer on MTV for the first time.

2003 The cheer team from the California School for the Deaf in Riverside, California, is the first deaf team to ever compete in the International Spirit Championships. They perform their routine to visual cues and placed first in their coed division!

Trivia

Cheerleading Chart Toppers

What do Christina Aguilera, Sandra Bullock, Cameron Diaz, and Madonna have in common? They were all high school cheerleaders!

What's the oldest stunt in cheerleading history? Probably the Cupie. In this classic partner stunt, the base holds the flyer's two feet high above his head using only one hand.

The first cheerleaders had to hand-make their pom-poms, crinkling flat strips of paper a few strips at a time. It took several hours to make just one!

Cheerleaders are smart. More than 80 percent have at least a B average in school and are leaders in student organizations.

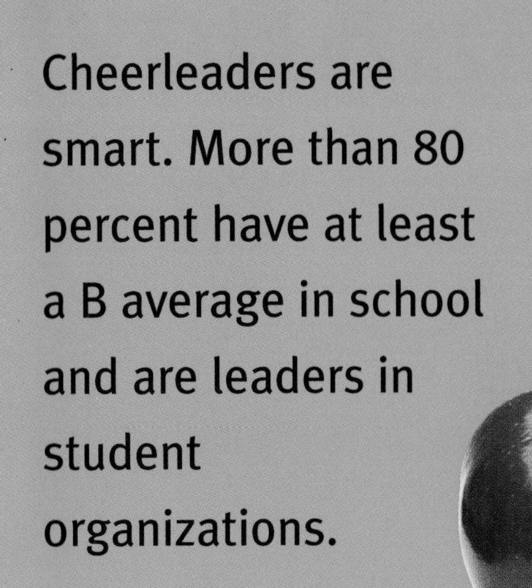

The Greenup County (Kentucky) High School cheerleading team is one of the top-rated high school squads in cheerleading history. They took home their first four national championships in 1981, 1982, 1983, and 1984. Then, they won five more. Now that's a record to beat!

More than 3 million boys and girls participate in cheerleading in the United States every year. Their average age is between 14 and 18 years old.

President George W. Bush participated in college cheerleading.

QUICK REFERENCE GUIDE

Cheerleading Words to Know

cartwheel: an acrobatic movement in which the feet turn over the hands

conditioning: the act of training the body for top physical performance

crowd cheer: a cheerleading shout in which the crowd joins in

formation: a specific lineup of cheerleaders that forms a certain shape or design

handspring: an acrobatic movement in which a cheerleader springs from feet to hands and back again in a forward or backward motion

megaphone: a cone-shaped device used to make the voice sound louder

mount cheer: a cheer that is recited as squad members climb upon each other's shoulders

pep rally: an event or gathering designed to boost school or team spirit

practice week: the period during which potential cheerleaders have an opportunity to learn the skills they will be tested on

pyramid: a cheerleading formation that resembles a three-dimensional triangle

ripple: a moving, wavelike variation of row height in a cheerleading formation

show cheer: an advanced cheer designed to engage audiences at competitions

spirit stick: a tubular device with colorful strings at each end, used as rewards and to rally fans

spotter: the person on the squad responsible for watching all parts of a stunt, especially the flyer

squad: another term for the cheerleading team

stunt: an intricate combination of cheerleading movements

tryouts: a period of time during which people compete for a spot on the squad

varsity: the main or best squad in any sport that is chosen to represent a school

GLOSSARY

Other Words to Know

Here are definitions for some of the words used in this book:

abdominal crunch: an exercise movement also known as a sit-up

aerial: a motion that occurs in mid-air

competition: a contest between rival or opposing teams

endurance: the ability to handle a long period of activity

enthusiasm: a feeling of excitement

flexibility: the ability to bend or move easily

foundation: the base on which something stands or is supported

fraternity: a men's student group formed for special activities; has a name made up of Greek letters

impact: the force of one object striking another

morale: the feelings of a group or person

projection: making something louder so it can be heard clearly

stretching: extending muscles

weight lifting: a sport or exercise designed to build strength

Where To Learn More

At the Library

French, Stephanie Breaux. *The Cheerleading Book.* Chicago: Contemporary Books, Inc., 1995.

Golden, Suzi J. *101 Best Cheers.* Mahwah, N.J.: Troll Communications, L.L.C., 2001.

Rusconi, Ellen. *Cheerleading.* Danbury, Conn.: Children's Press, 2001.

On the Road

Sam Houston State University
(home of the first cheerleading camp)
1802 Avenue I
Lowman Student Center
Huntsville, TX 77340
936/294-4239

Cheerleading Technique Camps
888/600-3178

On the Web

For more information on *cheerleading,* use FactHound to track down Web sites related to this book.

1. Go to www.compasspointbooks.com/facthound
2. Type in this book ID: 0756505844
3. Click on the *Fetch It* button.

Your trusty FactHound will fetch the best Web sites for you!

INDEX

aerials, 28–29, 47
American Association of Cheerleading Coaches and Advisors, 14
appearance, 13, 16

bases, 26–27
blades, 18
boys as cheerleaders, 6–7, 8, 16, 42, 45
breathing, 11

camps, 38–39, 42, 43, 47
cartwheels, 32, 46
chants, 34
cheers, 34–35, 40
clothing, 13, 16
coaches, 12, 14–15, 25, 31, 43
college cheerleaders, 43
competitions, 40, 43, 45, 47
conditioning programs, 14–15, 46. *See also* exercise.
crowd cheers, 35, 46

daggers, 19
dance, 8, 10

endurance, 10, 47
exercise, 10–11, 12, 28, 46

flexibility and stretching, 10, 22, 38, 47
flyers, 27, 28–29, 30–31
formations, 32–33, 40, 46
foundations, 26–27, 47

girls as cheerleaders, 7, 8, 16, 42, 45
gymnastics, 7, 8

handsprings, 32, 46
high V, 19, 22–23, 32
history of cheerleading, 6–7, 42–43

International Cheerleading Foundation, 14, 43

jumps, 13, 22–23

leadership, 9, 37, 43, 45
liberties (left and right), 21
low V, 19
lunges, 20, 32

megaphones, 17, 42, 46
mount cheers, 35, 46
moves in cheerleading, 18–21

National Cheerleaders Association, 14, 40, 42

pep rallies, 8, 36, 42, 46
pompoms, 17, 42, 44
practice week, 12, 46
preparations for cheerleading, 8–9
pyramids, 32, 46

ripples, 32, 46

show cheers, 35, 46
smiles, 4, 13, 38
spirit, 4, 8, 13, 36–37
spirit sticks, 42, 46
spotters, 16, 22, 25, 27, 30–31
squads, 4, 8, 12, 14–15, 16, 24–25, 31, 32–33, 36–37, 38–39, 40, 45, 46
strength, 10, 28. *See also* exercise.
stretching and flexibility, 10, 22, 47
stunts, 4, 15, 24–25, 26–27, 28–29, 30–31, 32–33, 40, 44, 46

teams. *See* squads.
transitions, 32
tryouts, 12, 13, 46

uniforms, 16
Universal Cheerleaders Association, 14, 40
University of Minnesota, 6–7, 42

voice projection, 11, 13, 47

About the Author

Beth Gruber has worked in children's book publishing for almost 20 years as an author, editor, and reviewer of many books for young readers. She also interviews other authors and TV show creators who write for children. Beth is a graduate of NYU School of Journalism. Reading and writing are her passions. She lives in New York City.